OCEANOGRAPHERS

PARKER HOLMES

PowerKiDS press.

New York

Published in 2016 by The Rosen Publishing Group, Inc.
29 East 21st Street, New York, NY 10010

First Edition

Editor: Katie Kawa
Designer: Mickey Harmon

Photo Credits: Cover Daniela Dirscherl/WaterFrame/Getty Images; p. 5 (main) Luis Lamar/Contributor/National Geographic/Getty Images; p. 5 (inset) https://en.wikipedia.org/wiki/HMS_Challenger_(1858)#/media/File:HMS_challenger_William_Frederick_Mitchell.jpg; pp. 6–7 Nick Gibson/age fotostock/Getty Images; pp. 8–9 Getty Images/Stringer/Getty Images News/Getty Images; pp. 10–11 StudioSmart/Shutterstock.com; p. 12 Cromagnon/Shutterstock.com; p. 13 SuperStock/SuperStock/Getty Images; p. 14 s_bukley/Shutterstock.com; p. 15 Thomas J. Abercrombie/Contributor/National Geographic/Getty Images; pp. 16, 17 Bates Littlehales/Contributor/National Geographic/Getty Images; pp. 18–19 Mark Conlin/Oxford Scientific/Getty Images; p. 21 (main) dmaster/Shutterstock.com; p. 21 (inset) https://commons.wikimedia.org/wiki/File:Echo_Sounding_of_Newly_Discovered_Canyon_in_the_Red_Sea_MOD_45155030.jpg; p. 22 (map) https://en.wikipedia.org/wiki/Meiji_Seamount#/media/File:EmperorSeamounts.jpg; pp. 22–23 nicolas.voisin44/Shutterstock.com; p. 25 https://upload.wikimedia.org/wikipedia/commons/3/3f/Exosuit_Back.jpg; p. 26 https://en.wikipedia.org/wiki/Giant_tube_worm#/media/File:Riftia_tube_worm_colony_Galapagos_2011.jpg; pp. 26–27 https://upload.wikimedia.org/wikipedia/commons/a/aa/Champagne_vent_white_smokers.jpg; pp. 28–29 Rich Carey/Shutterstock.com; p. 30 fenkieandreas/Shutterstock.com.

Cataloging-in-Publication Data

Holmes, Parker.
Oceanographers / by Parker Holmes.
p. cm. — (Out of the lab: extreme jobs in science)
Includes index.
ISBN 978-1-5081-4517-2 (pbk.)
ISBN 978-1-5081-4518-9 (6-pack)
ISBN 978-1-5081-4519-6 (library binding)
1. Oceanographers — Juvenile literature. 2. Oceanography — Vocational guidance — Juvenile literature. I. Holmes, Parker. II. Title.
GC30.5 H75 2016
551.46023—d23

Manufactured in the United States of America

CPSIA Compliance Information: Batch #BW16PK: For Further Information contact Rosen Publishing, New York, New York at 1-800-237-9932

Contents

UNDER THE SEA

Would you like to explore the ocean? Does diving to the bottom of the sea in a small submarine sound like fun? Maybe you'd like to come face to face with a giant shark or study coral reefs. These are the kinds of exciting things oceanographers do.

Oceanographers are scientists who study the ocean. They look at every part of the ocean—from giant underwater mountains to **microscopic** creatures. Some of these ocean scientists investigate how the ocean affects weather. Others research underwater volcanoes. Another kind of oceanographer might examine fish populations to find out if they're healthy.

Oceanographers study all kinds of mysteries of the deep sea. They've chosen a very cool career! Let's take a closer look at how these ocean scientists do their work.

SCIENCE IN ACTION

People have tried to understand the ocean since ancient times. However, the science of oceanography really took off in the 1870s. That's when the British ship the HMS *Challenger* sailed around the world studying the ocean. Many consider this the first true oceanography expedition.

The technology used by oceanographers has changed a lot since the days of the HMS *Challenger*. These scientists use the latest tools to study the most extreme parts of the ocean.

HMS CHALLENGER

A WET PLANET

About 71 percent of Earth is covered by ocean water. This water affects our lives in many ways. Ocean plants give us oxygen to breathe. Oceans provide us with fish to eat. Oceans also influence weather patterns.

There are five named oceans on our planet: the Pacific Ocean, the Atlantic Ocean, the Indian Ocean, the Arctic Ocean, and the Southern Ocean. Some oceanographers believe 95 percent of our oceans haven't been explored yet. Oceanographers still have a lot more to learn about the world's oceans. We have better maps of the planet Mars than we have of our own ocean floor! Studying oceans isn't easy because they're so deep. However, scientists are continuing to learn more about these great bodies of water.

SCIENCE IN ACTION

The Southern Ocean, which is sometimes called the Antarctic Ocean because it surrounds Antarctica, became the newest named ocean in 2000. Its waters used to be considered part of the Pacific Ocean, the Atlantic Ocean, and the Indian Ocean.

In this image of Earth taken from space, it's easy to see how much of our planet is covered by water. While there's actually only one global ocean, it's divided into five named oceans.

SOUTHERN OCEAN

TESTING THE WATERS

Different kinds of oceanographers do different jobs. Sometimes, they work out at sea, and they'll live on a ship for weeks. Other times, they analyze, or study, information in a computer lab.

Some oceanographers study the **geology** of the ocean floor. Did you know the ocean is full of mountains, canyons, and volcanoes? The largest known volcano on the planet is located in the Pacific Ocean! Scientists are still mapping the ocean floor. They want to understand how it was created and what it could look like in the future.

Other oceanographers research the movement of water. They look at tides, waves, and currents. Water movement affects weather, **erosion**, and other things on land. Their research can help keep us safe from **dangerous** storms.

SCIENCE IN ACTION

Scientists discovered that the longest mountain range on Earth is underwater. It's called the mid-ocean ridge, and it goes on for about 40,000 miles (64,373.8 km)!

We can sometimes see eruptions from underwater volcanoes, such as the one shown here. Oceanographers who study these volcanoes and other parts of the ocean floor are called geological oceanographers or marine geologists.

Oceanographers sometimes focus on chemistry. They want to understand the chemical makeup of seawater. They also study the ways chemicals dumped into the water through pollution can affect the ocean and the creatures that live in it.

Other oceanographers study the creatures that live underwater. As of 2015, more than 200,000 marine species have been named. Some scientists think millions of other **organisms** are waiting to be discovered—many of them too small to see without a microscope. Our oceans are full of life. Oceanographers want to know more about how all these creatures live.

During college, people who want to become oceanographers focus on different branches of science. They also need a good understanding of math, because much of the data they analyze is shown through numbers.

SCIENCE IN ACTION

Scientists who study sea creatures recently discovered a new species of underwater worms called "zombie worms." These worms feed on the bones of dead whales that sink to the bottom of the ocean. These worms are just one of the many kinds of cool creatures oceanographers study!

Branches of Science Studied by Oceanographers

branch of science	What does it focus on?	oceanography example
geophysics	the physical movements and forces on Earth	studying tides
geology	the history of Earth as shown through its rocks, soil, and landforms	studying the formation of mountains and volcanoes on the ocean floor
chemistry	the properties of substances and the changes they go through	analyzing the chemical composition of water around undersea volcanoes
biology	living things	researching new organisms found in seawater
environmental science	the interaction between living and nonliving things in terms of its impact on the environment	analyzing the effect of pollution on organisms that live in the ocean
engineering	the application of science and math in a way that's useful for people	designing new vehicles to travel to the ocean floor

People who want to become oceanographers generally study one of these branches of science in college. You need at least a four-year college degree to pursue a career in oceanography. Most oceanographers have more advanced college degrees.

TRIPS TO THE TRENCH

Imagine diving to the deepest part of the ocean. It's called the Mariana Trench. The trench is a huge crack on the floor of the Pacific Ocean. Its bottom is about 7 miles (11.3 km) underwater, which makes it the deepest known point on the planet. It's a place so cold, dark, and deep that—for many years—scientists didn't know if sea life could exist there.

However, oceanographers wanted to explore the Mariana Trench. No person had traveled there until scientists decided to try in 1960. Engineers built a **submersible** vessel that they hoped would be able to make the trip. They named it *Trieste*. Don Walsh of the United States Navy and Swiss oceanographer Jacques Piccard were chosen to make the trip into the trench in the *Trieste*.

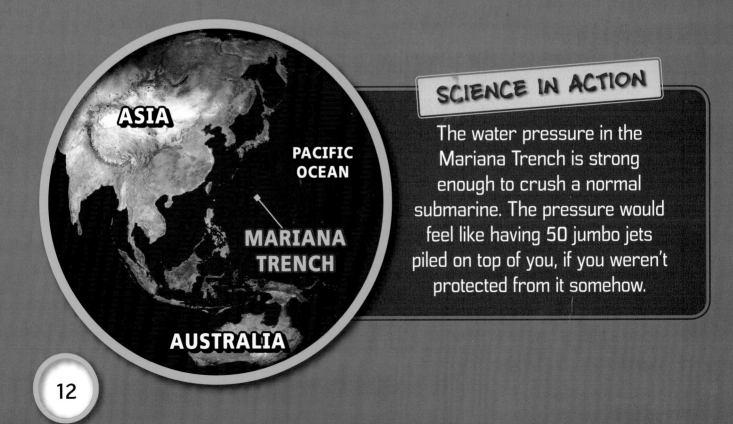

ASIA

PACIFIC OCEAN

MARIANA TRENCH

AUSTRALIA

SCIENCE IN ACTION

The water pressure in the Mariana Trench is strong enough to crush a normal submarine. The pressure would feel like having 50 jumbo jets piled on top of you, if you weren't protected from it somehow.

The *Trieste* was a bathyscaphe. This is a kind of submersible vessel with two main parts. The first is a cabin made of steel to resist water pressure. The second part is a float that has air tanks and gasoline tanks, so the vehicle can move on its own in the water.

Walsh and Piccard faced many dangers on their trip into the Mariana Trench. On their way down, they heard a strange noise. A window had cracked from the water pressure! Fortunately, they were able to keep going. It took them almost 5 hours to travel the 35,800 feet (10,911.8 m) to the bottom. Finally, they arrived.

Since that trip in 1960, oceanographers have sent other vessels down to the Mariana Trench. Scientists discovered life can exist at such extreme depths. In 2012, a filmmaker and deep-sea explorer named James Cameron traveled to an even deeper part of the trench than Walsh and Piccard. If you become an oceanographer, maybe you'll get to visit the trench yourself one day!

SCIENCE IN ACTION

James Cameron's interest in deep-sea travel has been a part of some of his most famous films. For his film *Titanic*, he made multiple trips into the ocean to view the remains of that sunken ship.

Cameron followed the example of Walsh and Piccard as he traveled to the bottom of the ocean in his vessel, the *DEEPSEA CHALLENGER*. Is that a trip you'd like to make?

JACQUES PICCARD

DON WALSH

LIVING UNDERWATER

Imagine waking up in the morning, looking out your window, and seeing a fish swim by. Is that really possible? Yes! Oceanographers have lived underwater. They've set up labs in the ocean so they can work, sleep, and even eat underwater.

Scientists figured out how to live underwater more than 50 years ago. They built labs that could be anchored to the sea floor. People could live inside them and breathe air. These labs allowed oceanographers to stay undersea for days—or even weeks—without going on dry land. This gave oceanographers a lot more time to do research.

Famous ocean explorer Jacques Cousteau helped design some of the first undersea labs. In 1962, a lab called Conshelf I was built. It allowed two people to live underwater for a week.

SCIENCE IN ACTION

Conshelf II was built in 1963. This was a bigger project than Conshelf I. It was like a village of underwater buildings. Conshelf III, shown here, was used in 1965 to house six people underwater for three weeks.

JACQUES COUSTEAU

Cousteau helped design many tools used by oceanographers, such as underwater cameras. His books, television programs, and films about the ocean increased people's interest in oceanography.

WHAT'S AQUARIUS?

Would you like to live underwater? For some oceanographers, it's a dream come true. The living conditions aren't always easy, though. You have to live in tight spaces with several other scientists. However, oceanographers who live underwater believe the work they're doing is exciting and important enough to make the crowded living spaces worthwhile.

Some oceanographers now work out of an undersea lab called Aquarius, which was first used in 1993. It sits about 63 feet (19.2 m) underwater off the **Florida Keys**. Aquarius is used for underwater missions lasting up to 10 days. Inside the lab, oceanographers have beds, a bathroom, a microwave, and air conditioning. Aquarius also has computers to help oceanographers analyze and share their research directly from the water.

SCIENCE IN ACTION

Oceanographers who live and work inside and outside an underwater lab for a period of time are sometimes called aquanauts or oceanauts.

Aquarius uses advanced technology to allow oceanographers to live and work underwater for days at a time. It's one of the most extreme places to work on the planet!

MODERN TECHNOLOGY

A century ago, oceanographers could never have explored the Mariana Trench or lived underwater. Now, oceanographers are using the latest technology to learn as much as possible about this undersea world.

Measuring water depth used to be difficult. Oceanographers dropped a heavy weight, which was attached to a long rope, over the side of a ship. They waited for the weight to hit bottom. Then, they pulled the weight back up. The rope was marked with flags to get more **accurate** measurements. However, it was still hard to get a true measurement of depth using this method.

Later on, scientists discovered a much better way: sonar. A sonar machine can send sound waves to the ocean floor. Scientists can then figure out depth based on how long it takes the sound waves to **echo** back from the bottom.

SCIENCE IN ACTION

The deepest part of the Mariana Trench is called Challenger Deep. It's named after the HMS *Challenger*, on which oceanographers first tried to measure the depth of the trench in 1875 using miles of rope.

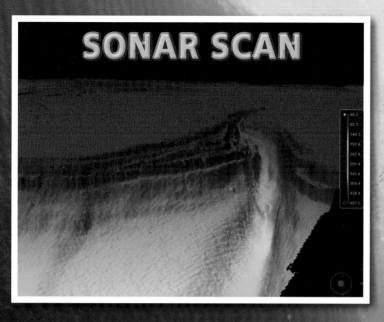

SONAR SCAN

46.3
96.3
144.3
193.4
242.4
291.4
340.4
389.4
438.4
487.5

Just like Earth's surface, oceans have mountains, valleys, canyons, and plains. Some of the deepest canyons on the planet are underwater! With sonar, oceanographers can learn what the ocean floor looks like.

SATELLITES AND SCUBA GEAR

Oceanographers use sonar to map the **topography** of the ocean floor. They also use **satellites** in space to map oceans. Satellites detect changes in sea levels by detecting changes in gravity underwater. This allows oceanographers to create more accurate maps of the ocean floor.

Scuba equipment is another important tool for oceanographers. Scuba equipment allows people to stay underwater and breathe air from a tank on their back. Using this technology, oceanographers can observe sea creatures, such as hammerhead sharks or coral, for longer periods of time. Does that sound like fun to you?

If oceanographers want to dive much deeper, they need special equipment. The water pressure at extreme depths is too strong for regular scuba diving. The pressure could kill a person without the proper gear.

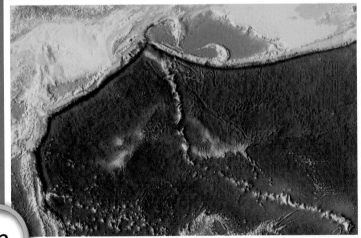

SATELLITE OCEAN MAP

Scuba equipment allows oceanographers to study the ocean up close. Satellites allow them to study the ocean from far way.

SCIENCE IN ACTION

The word "scuba" comes from the **acronym** "SCUBA," which stands for "Self-Contained Underwater Breathing Apparatus." You don't have to be an oceanographer to go scuba diving, but you do need to take special classes to learn to scuba dive.

DIVING DEEPER

In extremely deep water, divers put on suits that look like armor. The suits are made of strong materials that protect divers from the extreme water pressure. The full name of this kind of suit is an atmospheric diving system (ADS). The famous oceanographer Sylvia Earle used one of these suits in 1979 to walk on the ocean floor at a depth of 1,250 feet (381 m).

What if you want to go even deeper? Then you need to travel in a submersible vessel. That's what was used in 1960 to dive to the bottom of the Mariana Trench. Sometimes oceanographers are inside the submersible vessel. Other times, no one is in it, and it's remote controlled. Submersible vessels often have cameras and equipment for research. Remote-controlled submersibles have discovered deep-sea creatures never seen before!

SCIENCE IN ACTION

Oceanographers who travel deep underwater have to worry about decompression sickness. This happens when people go from a high-pressure environment to a low-pressure one too quickly and bubbles form inside their body. People who have decompression sickness often have pain in their **joints**. Sometimes, it can lead to heart, lung, or brain problems.

An ADS allows oceanographers to go up to 1,000 feet (304.8 m) underwater without suffering from decompression sickness. The back of an ADS is shown here.

CREATURES BIG AND SMALL

What's the most extreme place on the planet where life exists? It may be hydrothermal vents. These are holes in the deep ocean floor that spew **fluids** that can be as hot as 700 degrees Fahrenheit (371 degrees Celsius). The fluids that come out of hydrothermal vents are so hot they would melt your skin! However, oceanographers discovered that some types of sea life actually exist around the vents. These vents may give scientists clues about early life on Earth.

Oceanographers investigate all kinds of sea creatures. They study creatures as large as blue whales and as small as microorganisms. A microorganism is a living thing that's so small it can only be seen with a microscope. Scientists think the ocean contains so many microorganisms that they weigh more than all the fish put together!

TUBE WORMS

SCIENCE IN ACTION

An extremophile is any living thing that lives in extreme surroundings, such as the intense heat around a hydrothermal vent. Tube worms are one example of extremophiles that call a hydrothermal vent home.

Hydrothermal vents are found deep in the ocean, in total darkness. They can only be seen by oceanographers using submersible vessels.

A HEALTHY PLANET

Oceanographers have a very important job. We all rely on oceans in some way, so scientists need to learn as much as they can about these bodies of water.

Some people used to think oceans were so big they couldn't be damaged. Now, we know that's not true. That's why oceanographers are trying to protect our seas. They're looking at how pollution might be killing coral reefs and other sea life. They're studying how overfishing could destroy some fish populations. They're also trying to figure out how our climate is changing. If oceans grow warmer, it can harm marine life and change the weather. Hotter temperatures also raise sea levels, which could flood cities. Oceanographers are closely measuring water temperatures and sea levels for this reason.

SCIENCE IN ACTION

Hurricanes are powerful storms created over warm ocean water. Oceanographers help us better understand how hurricanes form.

Oceanographers are doing their part to protect sea creatures and the oceans they call home. They're studying the ways people have changed oceans and what can be done to stop those changes from causing more damage.

EXPLORING THE SEAS

A career in oceanography can be an adventure. You can dive with great white sharks. You can travel around the world on a ship. You can even ride in submersible vessels to the bottom of the sea. However, if you'd rather stay on dry land, you can still work as an oceanographer. Some oceanographers spend their time in labs using microscopes and computers. There are many careers to choose from in the field of oceanography.

Oceans are like wild frontiers for oceanographers to explore. They're full of surprises! One day, you might discover a new creature on the dark bottom of the sea. The next day, you might find a new underwater volcano. There's a world of wonder and mystery to be found underwater. Would you like to help explore it by becoming an oceanographer?

GLOSSARY

accurate: Free of mistakes.

acronym: A word formed from the first letters of each one of the words in a phrase.

dangerous: Not safe.

echo: To send back a reflection of sound waves.

erosion: The wearing away of land, such as a shore being washed away by water.

Florida Keys: A group of small islands off the southern coast of Florida between the Atlantic Ocean and the Gulf of Mexico.

fluid: A substance that flows freely like water.

geology: The scientific study of the history of Earth as shown through its rocks, soil, and landforms.

joint: A point where two bones meet in the body.

microscopic: So small it can only be seen with a microscope.

organism: An individual living thing.

satellite: A spacecraft that is sent into orbit to gather information.

submersible: Able to be used underwater.

topography: The physical or natural features of an area, such as mountains and canyons.

INDEX

WEBSITES

Due to the changing nature of Internet links, PowerKids Press has developed an online list of websites related to the subject of this book. This site is updated regularly. Please use this link to access the list:

www.powerkidslinks.com/exsci/ocean